WARNER BROS. PRESENTS
MELLOW ROCK CLASSICS

Editor: Carol Cuellar
Cover Design: Richard Chimelis

ISBN 0-89724-606-3

CONTENTS

CONTENTS

DESPERADO

Words and Music by
DON HENLEY and GLENN FREY

6

day._____ You're los - in' all__ your highs__ and lows.__ Ain't it

fun - ny how__ the feel - in' goes__ a - way?_____

Des - per - a - do, why don't__ you

come to your sens - es? Come down from your fenc - es,__

ANOTHER DAY IN PARADISE

Words and Music by
PHIL COLLINS

Another Day in Paradise - 4 - 1

12

VERSE 2:
He walks on, doesn't look back,
He pretends he can't hear her,
Starts to whistle as he crosses the street,
Seems embarrased to be there.

VERSE 3:
She calls out to the man on the street,
He can see she's been crying,
She's got blisters on the soles of her feet,
She can't walk, but she's trying.

VERSE 4: (%)
You can tell from the lines on her face,
You can see that she's been there,
Probably been moved on from every place,
'Cos she didn't fit in there.

DO I HAVE TO SAY THE WORDS?

Lyrics and Music by
BRYAN ADAMS & JIM VALLANCE
& R.J. LANGE

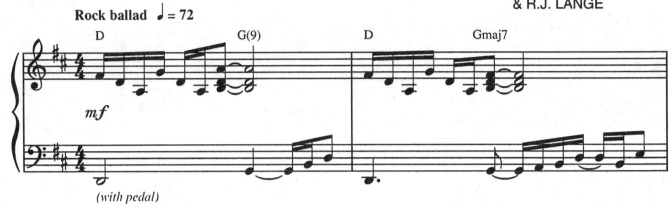

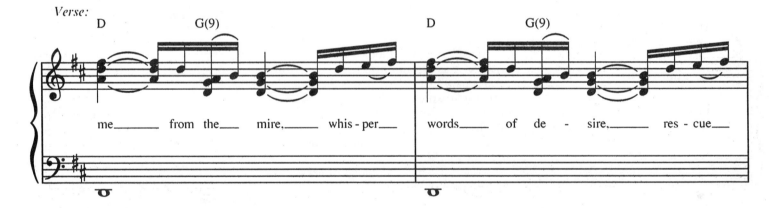

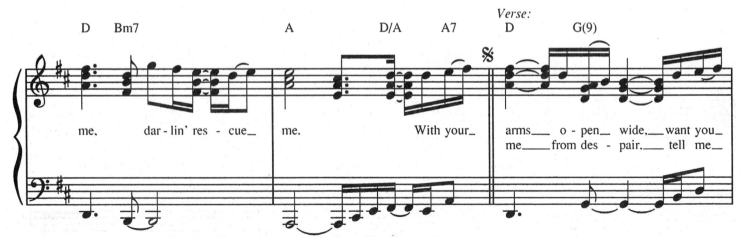

Do I Have to Say the Words? - 4 - 1

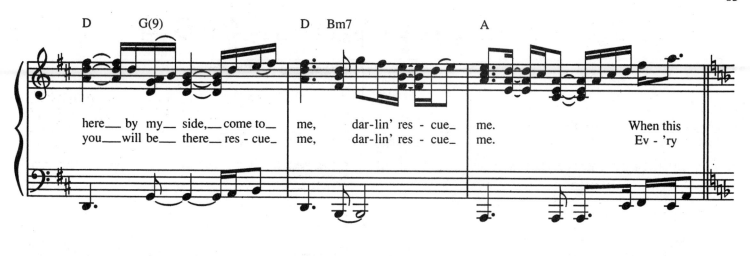

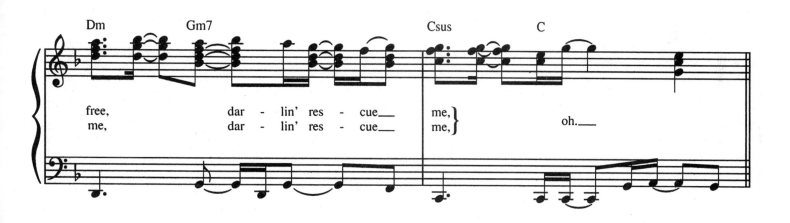

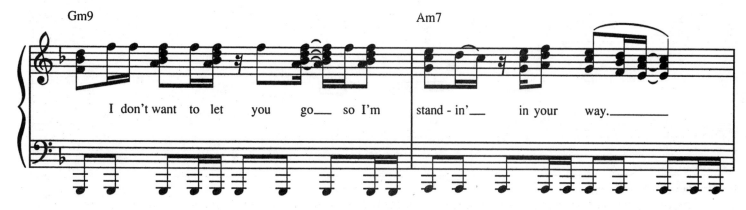

Do I Have to Say the Words? - 4 - 2

DOWN ON THE CORNER

Words and Music by
JOHN C. FOGERTY

FAITHFULLY

Slow rock ♩ = 66

Words and Music by
JONATHAN CAIN

Faithfully - 4 - 1

Rest - less hearts sleep a - lone to - night, ___ sendin' all ___ my love ___ a - long the wire. _____ They say that the road ain't no ___ place to start a fam- 'ly.

Right down the line ___ it's been you and me. ___

And lov-in' a mu-sic man ain't al-ways what it's s'pposed to be. Oh girl, you stand by me. I'm for-ev-er yours, faith-ful-ly. (Instrumental Solo)

(end solo)   2. Cir-cus

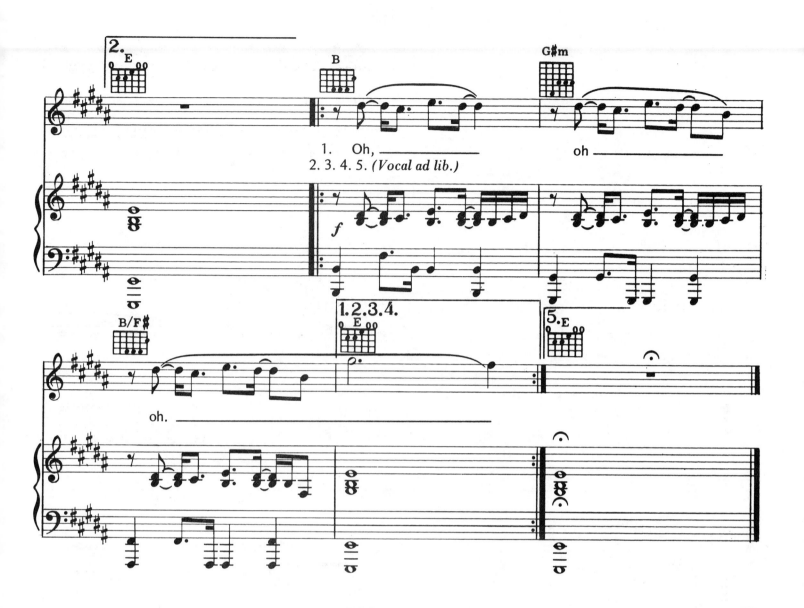

1. Oh, _____
2. 3. 4. 5. *(Vocal ad lib.)*

oh _____

oh. _____

Verse 2:
Circus life
Under the big top world;
We all need the clowns
To make us smile.
Through space and time
Always another show.
Wondering where I am;
Lost without you.

And being apart ain't easy
On this love affair;
Two strangers learn to fall
In love again.
I get the joy
Of rediscovering you.
Oh girl, you stand by me.
I'm forever yours, faithfully.

AFRICA

Words and Music by
DAVID PAICH and JEFF PORCARO

Africa - 6 - 1

ech - o - in' to-night.___ She hears on - ly whis - pers of some

qui - et con - ver - sa - tion.

She's com - ing in, twelve thir - ty flight.___
The wild dogs cry out in the night,___ as

Moon - lit wings___ re - flect the stars___ that guide me toward___ sal -
they grow rest - less, long - ing for___ some sol - i - tar - y

Africa - 6 - 2

Repeat and fade

Africa - 6 - 6

I'LL HAVE TO SAY I LOVE YOU IN A SONG

Words and Music by
JIM CROCE

I'll Have to Say I Love You in a Song - 2 - 1

I'll Have to Say I Love You in a Song - 2 - 2

MEXICO

Words and Music by
JAMES TAYLOR

DON'T LOSE MY NUMBER

Words and Music by
PHIL COLLINS

Don't Lose My Number - 6 - 1

39

Don't Lose My Number - 6 - 4

oh Bil - ly, you _ bet - ter, you_

_ bet-ter, you _ bet-ter run _ for your life._

Bil - ly, Bil - ly don't you lose my num - ber,

RIDERS ON THE STORM

Words and Music by
THE DOORS

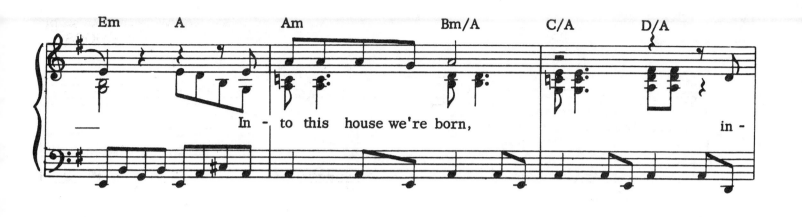

In - to this house we're born, in -

to this world we're thrown like a dog with - out a bone, an

act - or out on loan. Ri - ders on the storm. _____ There's a

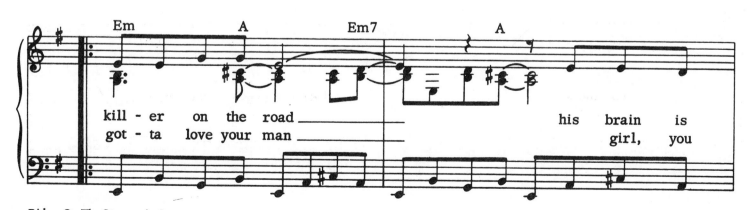

kill - er on the road _____ his brain is
got - ta love your man _____ girl, you

Riders On The Storm - 4 - 2

squirm-ing like a toad. _____ Take a long hol-i day
got - ta love your man. _____ Take him by the hand

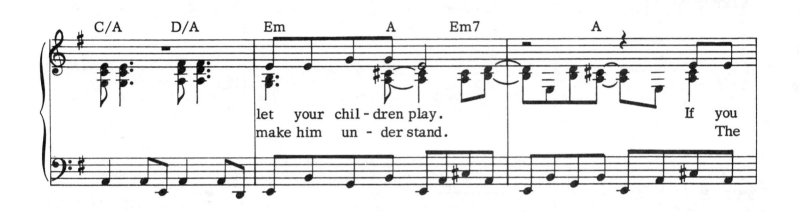

let your chil-dren play. If you
make him un - der stand. The

give this man a ride, sweet fam-i - ly will die. Kill-er on the road. _____
world on you de-pends, our life will nev-er end. You got-ta love your man. _____

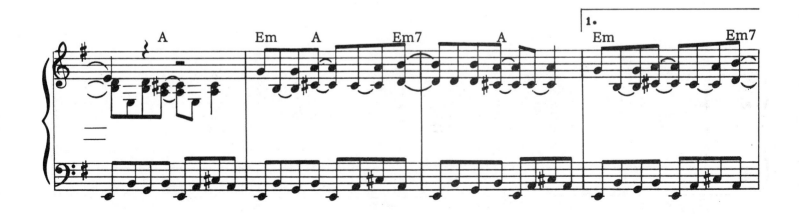

Riders On The Storm - 4 - 4

Repeat and fade

ROSIE

Words and Music by
JACKSON BROWNE and DONALD MILLER

Rosie - 4 - 1

Rosie - 4 - 2

ROUGH BOY

Words and Music by
BILLY GIBBONS, DUSTY HILL
and FRANK BEARD

Rough Boy - 4 - 1

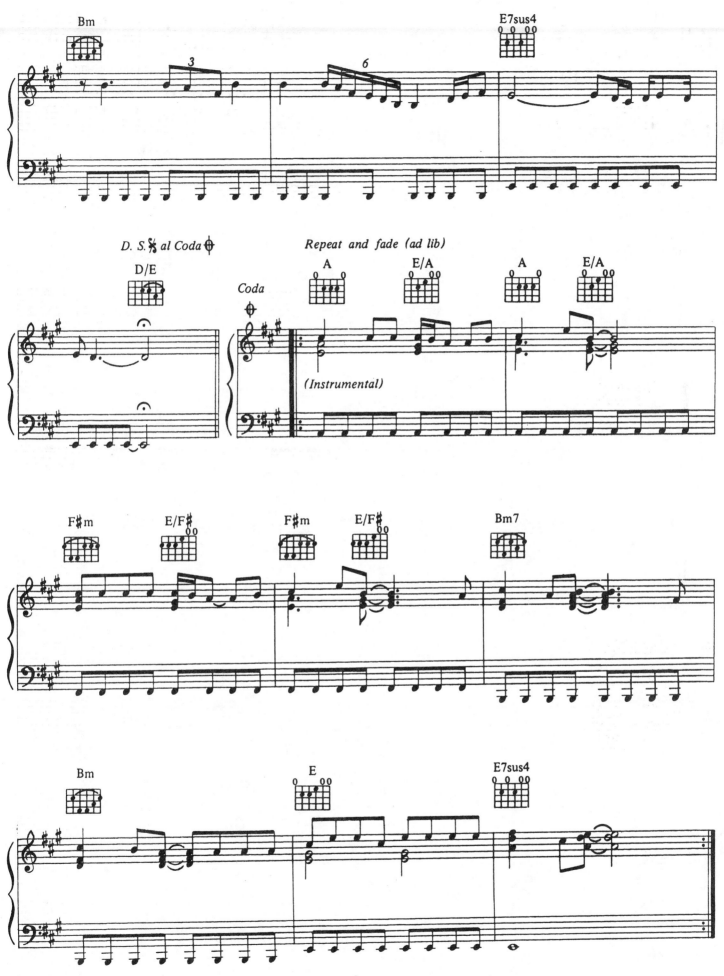

Rough Boy - 4 - 4

THE HEART OF THE MATTER

Words and Music by
DON HENLEY, MIKE CAMPBELL
and J.D. SOUTHER

Moderately slow

I got the call __ to- day, I didn't want to hear __ but I knew that it __ would come. __
(See additional lyrics)

An old, __ true friend of ours __ was talk- in' on __ the phone, __ she said you

The Heart of the Matter - 6 - 1

found some - one. And I thought of all — the bad — luck and the

strug - gles we went — through — and how I lost me — and you lost you. —

What are — these voi - ces out - side love's — o - pen door, make us throw off our con - tent - ment and

beg for some - thing more? — I'm learn - ing to live — with - out — you now, —

The Heart of the Matter - 6 - 3

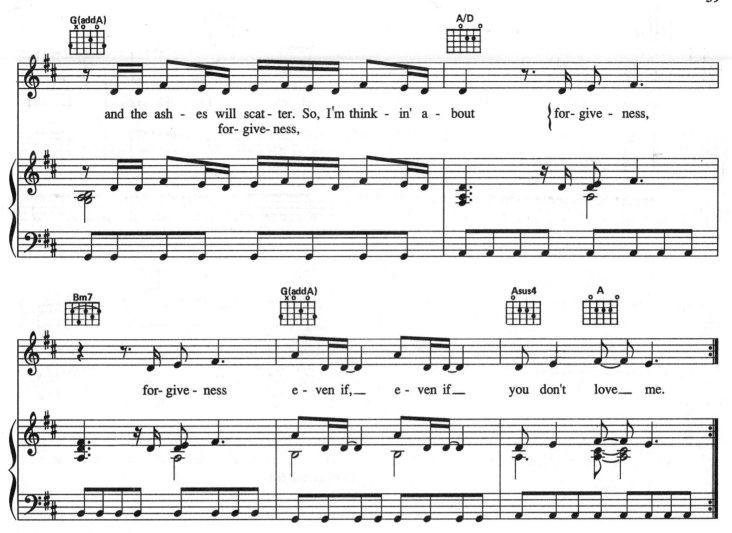

and the ash - es will scat - ter. So, I'm think - in' a - bout {for - give - ness,
for - give - ness,

for - give - ness e - ven if,__ e - ven if__ you don't love__ me.

Additional Lyrics

Verse 2:   These times are so uncertain
There's a yearning undefined
... people filled with rage
We all need a little tenderness
How can love survive in such a graceless age?
The trust and self-assurance that lead to happiness
They're the very things we kill, I guess
Pride and competition
    cannot fill these empty arms
And the work I put between us
    doesn't keep me warm

Chorus 2:   I'm learning to live without you now
But I miss you, baby
The more I know, the less I understand
All the things I **thought** I'd figured out
I have to learn again
I've been trying to get down
    to the heart of the matter
But everything changes
    and my friends seem to scatter
But I think it's about forgiveness
Forgiveness
Even if, even if you don't love me anymore.

The Heart of the Matter - 6 - 6

TRUCKIN'

Words by
ROBERT HUNTER

Music by
JERRY GARCIA, BOB WEIR
and PHIL LESH

Truckin' - 10 - 1

Ar-rows of ne-on and flash-ing mar-quees out on Main Street,— Chi-
Most of the cats that you meet on the street speak of true love.—

ca-go, New York, De-troit, and it's all on the same street.— Your
Most of the time they're sit-tin' and cry-in' at home.

typ-i-cal cit-y in-volved in a typ-i-cal day-dream,—
One of these days they know they got-ta get go-in'——

hang it up and see what to-mor-row brings.—
out of the door and down to the street all a-lone.

Truckin' - 10 - 3

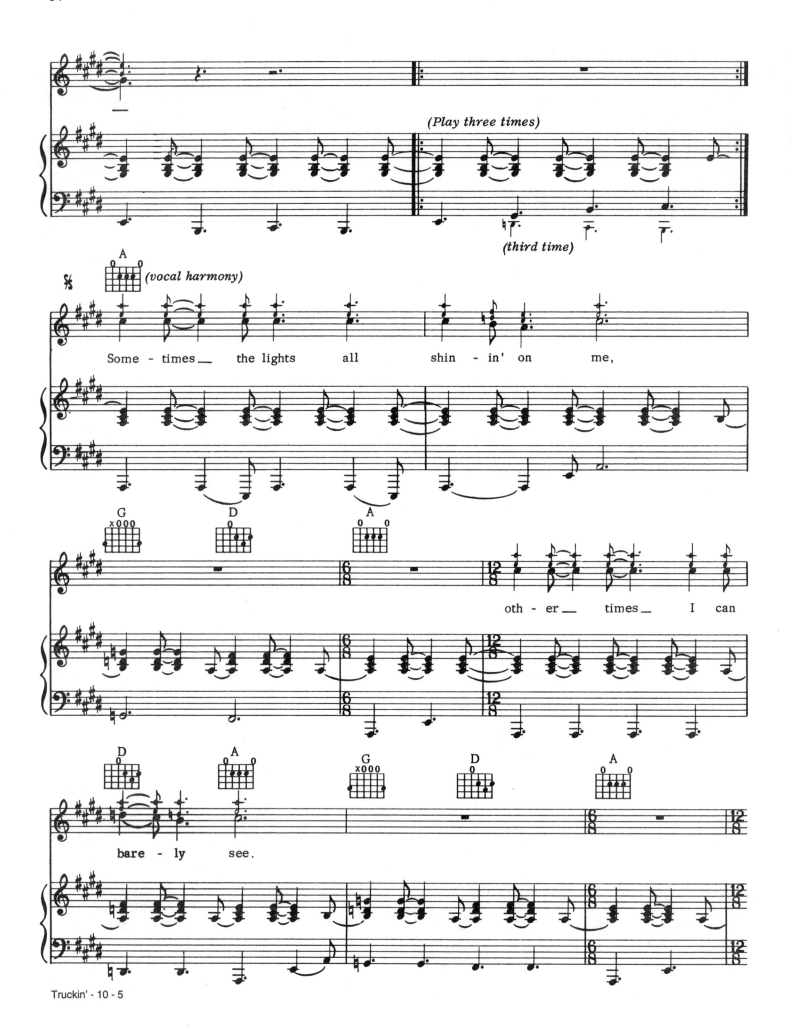

(Play three times)

(third time)

(vocal harmony)

Some - times___ the lights all shin - in' on me,

oth - er ___ times ___ I can

bare - ly see.

ROUGH BOY

Words and Music by
BILLY GIBBONS, DUSTY HILL
and FRANK BEARD

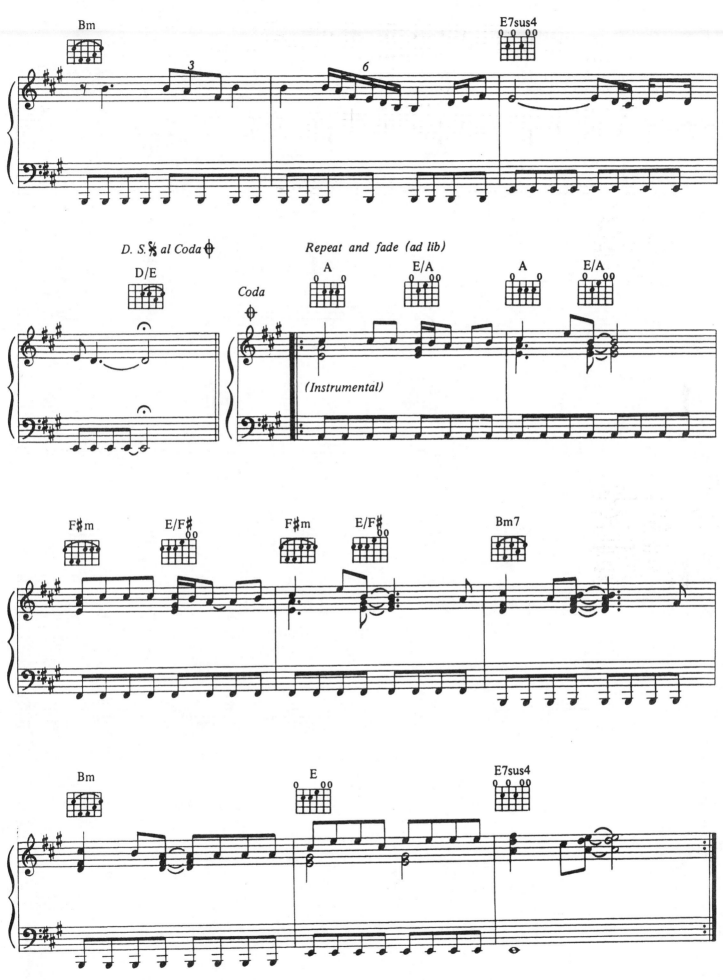

Rough Boy - 4 - 4

THE HEART OF THE MATTER

Words and Music by
DON HENLEY, MIKE CAMPBELL
and J.D. SOUTHER

I got the call _ to-day, I didn't want to hear _ but I knew that it _ would come. _
(See additional lyrics)

An old, _ true friend of ours _ was talk-in' on _ the phone, _ she said you

The Heart of the Matter - 6 - 1

The Heart of the Matter - 6 - 3

58

The Heart of the Matter - 6 - 5

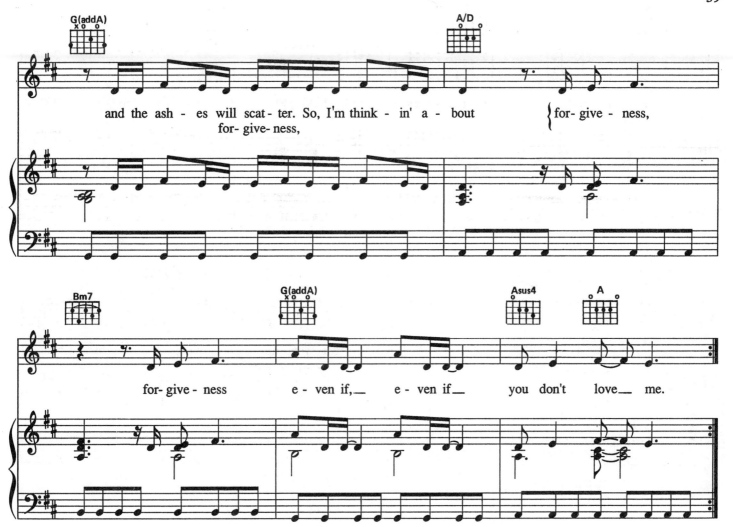

and the ash - es will scat - ter. So, I'm think - in' a - bout for- give - ness, for- give - ness,

for- give - ness   e - ven if,__   e - ven if__   you don't   love__ me.

Additional Lyrics

Verse 2:

These times are so uncertain
There's a yearning undefined
... people filled with rage
We all need a little tenderness
How can love survive in such a graceless age?
The trust and self-assurance that lead to happiness
They're the very things we kill, I guess
Pride and competition
   cannot fill these empty arms
And the work I put between us
   doesn't keep me warm

Chorus 2:

I'm learning to live without you now
But I miss you, baby
The more I know, the less I understand
All the things I **thought** I'd figured out
I have to learn again
I've been trying to get down
   to the heart of the matter
But everything changes
   and my friends seem to scatter
But I think it's about forgiveness
Forgiveness
Even if, even if you don't love me anymore.

The Heart of the Matter - 6 - 6

TRUCKIN'

Words by
ROBERT HUNTER

Music by
JERRY GARCIA, BOB WEIR
and PHIL LESH

Truckin' - 10 - 1

Ar-rows of ne - on and flash - ing mar-quees out on Main Street, _ Chi-
Most of the cats that you meet on the street speak of true love. _

ca - go, New York, De - troit, and it's all on the same street. _ Your
Most of the time they're sit - tin' and cry - in' at home.

typ - i - cal cit - y in-volved in a typ - i - cal day - dream, _
One of these days they know they got - ta get go - in' _

hang it up and see what to - mor-row brings. _
out of the door and down to the street all a - lone.

64

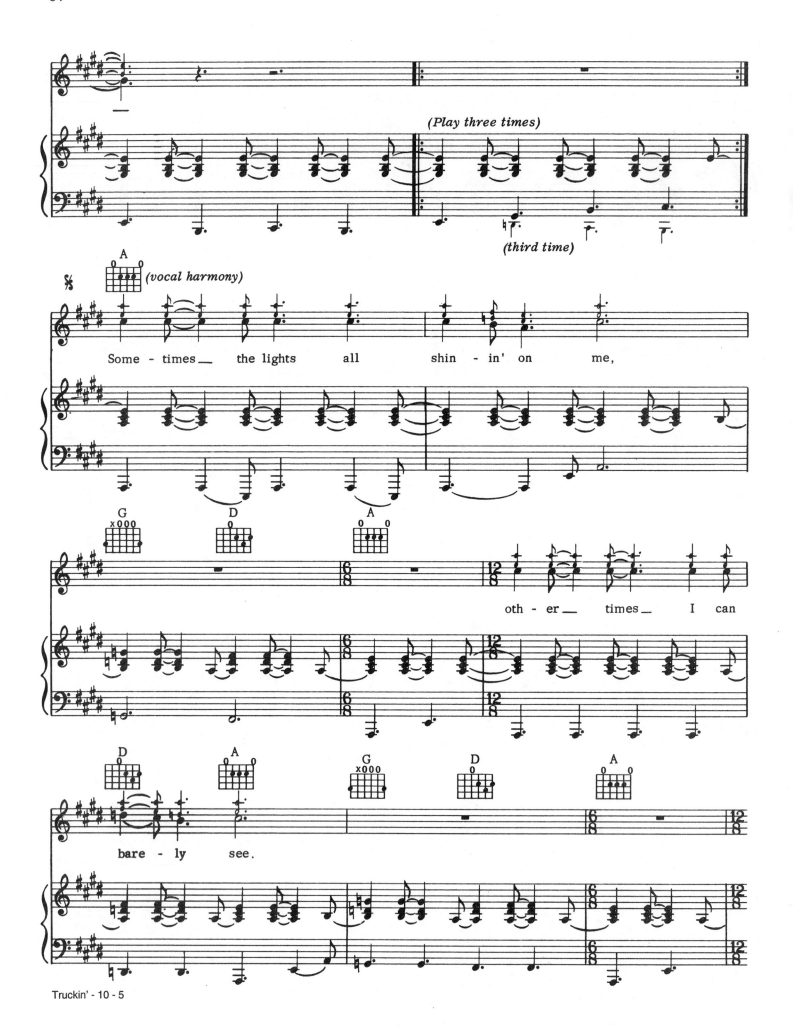

Truckin' - 10 - 6

E

What in the world ev-er be-came of sweet Jane?___ She
Sit-tin' and star-in' out of the ho-tel win-dow,___

lost her spar-kle; you know she is-n't the same.
got a tip they're gon-na kick the door in a-gain. I'd

Liv-in' on reds, vi-ta-min C___ and co-caine,___
like to get some sleep be-fore___ I trav-el,___ but if

all a friend can say is, "Ain't it a shame."___
you got a war-rant I guess you're gon-na come in.___

WHAT A FOOL BELIEVES

Words and Music by
KENNY LOGGINS and
MICHAEL McDONALD

Moderately bright, lightly

74

What a Fool Believes - 6 - 6

WHEN THE NIGHT COMES

Lyrics and Music by
BRYAN ADAMS, JIM VALLANCE
& DIANE WARREN

When The Night Comes - 4 - 1

Chorus:

Bridge:

B♭m   D♭   B♭m

I know there'll be a time for you and I, just take my hand and run a-

D♭   E♭m

way. Pick up__ all the piec-es__ of this

B♭m   G♭

shat-tered dream,__ we're gon-na make it ours__ some-day. That's when we're

D.S. 𝄋

A♭

com-in' back,__ com-in' back to stay._____

Verse 2:
Two spirits in the night,
We could leave before the morning light.
When there's nothin' left to lose,
There's nothin' left to fear.
So meet me on the edge of town.
Won't keep you waitin', I'll be 'round.
Then, you and I, we'll just roll right outa here.
To Chorus:

Verse 3: (Instrumental Solo)
To Chorus:

When The Night Comes - 4 - 4

WORKIN' AT THE CAR WASH BLUES

Words and Music by
JIM CROCE

Moderately, with a funky beat

Well, I had just got out from the coun-ty pris-on, do-in' nine-ty days for non-sup-port.

Tried to find me an ex-ec-u-tive po-si-tion but no mat-ter how smooth I talked

They would-n't lis-ten to the fact that I was a ge-nius, the man say, "We got all that we can use."

Workin' At the Car Wash Blues - 4 - 1

Workin' At the Car Wash Blues - 4 - 2

Workin' At the Car Wash Blues - 4 - 4

WITCHY WOMAN

Words and Music by
BERNIE LEADON & DON HENLEY

Witchy Woman - 4 - 1

Witchy Woman - 4 - 4

EASY LOVER

Words by
PHIL COLLINS

Music by
PHILIP BAILEY, PHIL COLLINS
and NATHAN EAST

Eas - y lov - er. She'll get a hold on you, be - lieve — it,

Easy Lover - 4 - 1

Easy Lover - 4 - 4

BAD MOON RISING

Words and Music by
J.C. FOGERTY

CASEY JONES

Words by
ROBERT HUNTER

Music by
JERRY GARCIA

Casey Jones - 6 - 1

Casey Jones - 6 - 2

Casey Jones - 6 - 4

HEAVEN

Words and Music by
BRYAN ADAMS and
JIM VALLANCE

1. Oh, think-in' a-bout all our young-er years; there was
2. Oh, once in your life you will find some-one who will

on-ly you and me; we were young and wild and free.
turn your world a-round; bring you up when you're feel-ing down.

Heaven - 4 - 1

I CAN'T TELL YOU WHY

Words and Music by
DON HENLEY, GLENN FREY & TIMOTHY B. SCHMIT

I Can't Tell You Why - 4 - 2

I DON'T CARE ANYMORE

Words and Music by
PHIL COLLINS

Well you can tell ev-'ry-one I'm a down —— dis - grace. ——
talk-ing to the peo-ple that you call your friends —— and it
-mem-ber all the times I tried —— so hard —— and you

Drag my —— name all —— o - ver the place. — I don't
seems to —— me there's a means to an end.—They don't } care an-y-more.
laughed in my face 'cos you held all the cards.— I don't

I Don't Care Anymore - 4 - 1

I Don't Care Anymore - 4 - 2

I Don't Care Anymore - 4 - 4

111

From the Twentieth Century Fox Motion Picture "THE LAST AMERICAN HERO"

I GOT A NAME

Words by
NORMAN GIMBEL

Music by
CHARLES FOX

I Got a Name - 4 - 1

I Got a Name - 4 - 2

I Got a Name - 4 - 4

LATE FOR THE SKY

Words and Music by
JACKSON BROWNE

Late for the Sky - 4 - 1

LYIN' EYES

Words and Music by
DON HENLEY & GLENN FREY

Lyin' Eyes - 6 - 1

Lyin' Eyes - 6 - 4

MISUNDERSTANDING

Words and Music by
PHIL COLLINS

Misunderstanding - 4 - 1

128 C

ONE MORE NIGHT

Words and Music by
PHIL COLLINS

One More Night - 6 - 1

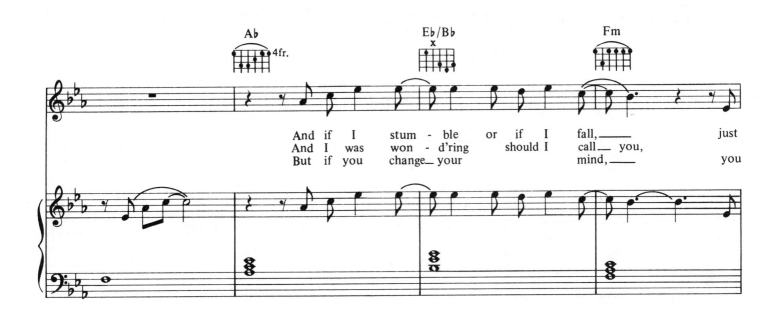

PROUD MARY

Words and Music by
J. C. FOGERTY

Proud Mary - 2 - 1

TEARS IN HEAVEN

Moderately slow ♩ = 80

Words and Music by
WILL JENNINGS and ERIC CLAPTON

TAKE ME HOME

Words and Music by
PHIL COLLINS

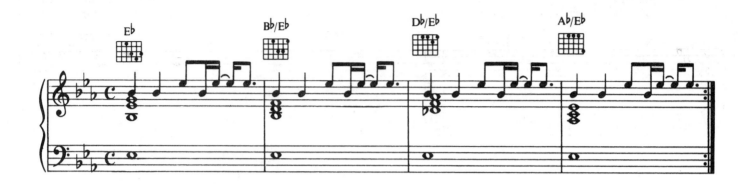

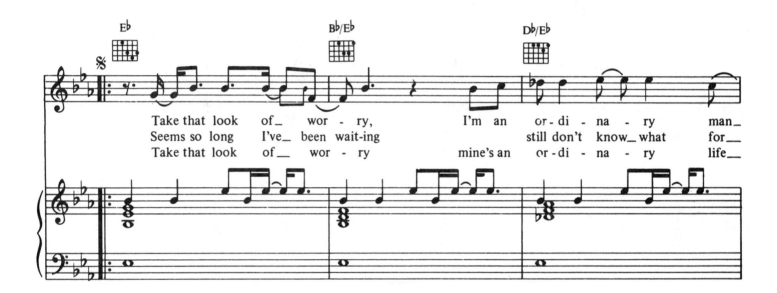

Take that look of___ wor - ry, I'm an or - di - na - ry man___
Seems so long I've___ been wait-ing still don't know___ what for___
Take that look of___ wor - ry mine's an or - di - na - ry life___

___ they___don't tell___ me no - thing so I
___ there's no point___ es - cap - ing I don't
___ work - ing when___ it's___ day - light and

Take Me Home - 6 - 1

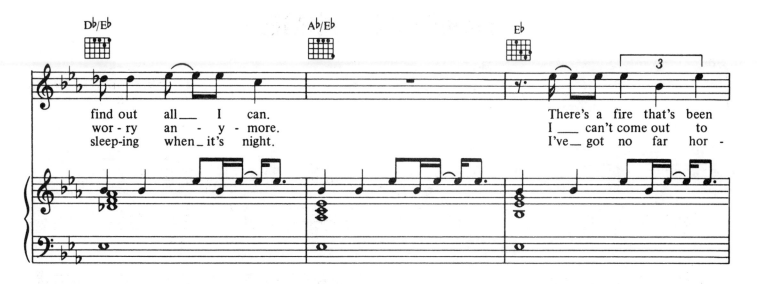

Db/Eb   Ab/Eb   Eb

find out all___ I can.
wor - ry an___ y - more.
sleep-ing when__ it's night.

There's a fire that's been
I ___ can't come out to
I've__ got no far hor -

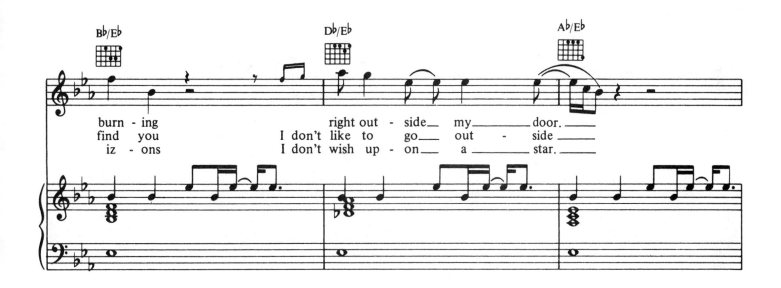

Bb/Eb   Db/Eb   Ab/Eb

burn - ing   right out - side__ my_____ door.____
find you   I don't like to go__ out - side _____
iz - ons   I don't wish up - on__ a _____ star.____

Eb   Bb/Eb   Db/Eb

I __ can't see but I   feel it   and it helps to keep__ me   warm.
They can turn off my   feel-ings   like they're turn - ing off__ the   light.
They don't think that I lis - ten   oh but I know who__ they   are.__

Take Me Home - 6 - 2

ber, ___ take, take ___ me home

oh no, ___ 'cause I've been a prison-er all ___ my life ___

— and I can say to you, ___ but I don't re - mem - ber ___

Repeat to Fade

take, take ___ me home 'cause I don't re - mem-

Take Me Home - 6 - 6

YOU DON'T MESS AROUND WITH JIM

Words and Music by
JIM CROCE

You Don't Mess around with Jim - 6 - 1

You Don't Mess around with Jim - 6 - 2

Well out-a south Al-a-bam-a come a coun-try boy. He said, "I'm look-in' for a man named Jim,___ I am a pool shoot-in' boy, my name is Wil-lie Mc-Coy___ but down home they call me Slim.___ Yeah, I'm look-in' for the king of For-ty-

IN THE AIR TONIGHT

Words and Music by
PHIL COLLINS

RUNNING ON EMPTY

Words and Music by
JACKSON BROWNE

Running on Empty - 8 - 1

164

Ev-'ry-one I know,___ ev-'ry-where I go,___

TOP HAT BAR AND GRILLE

Words and Music by
JIM CROCE

Top Hat Bar and Grille - 4 - 1

Top Hat Bar and Grille - 4 - 2

Top Hat Bar and Grille - 4 - 4

From the Motion Picture Soundtrack ''BUSTER''

TWO HEARTS

Words by
PHIL COLLINS

Music by
LAMONT DOZIER

Two Hearts - 6 - 1

Additional Lyrics

Well there's no easy way to, to understand it.
There's so much of my life in her
And it's like I planned it.
And it teaches you to never let go,
There's so much love you'll never know.
She can reach you no matter how far,
Wherever you are.

Two Hearts - 6 - 6

178

BACK IN THE HIGH LIFE AGAIN

Words and Music by
STEVE WINWOOD and WILL JENNINGS

Back in the High Life Again - 5 - 1

Back in the High Life Again - 5 - 2

182

BAD, BAD LEROY BROWN

Words and Music by
JIM CROCE

Bad, Bad Leroy Brown - 3 - 1

184

Bad, Bad Leroy Brown - 3 - 2

Bad, Bad Leroy Brown - 3 - 3

THE BEST OF MY LOVE

Words and Music by
DON HENLEY, GLENN FREY
and JOHN DAVID SOUTHER

Moderately slow

mp legato

with pedal throughout

Ev - er - y night __ I'm ly - in' in bed, __ hold-in' you close __ in my

Beau - ti - ful faces and loud emp - ty places, look at the way that we

dreams; __ think-in' a bout all the things that we __ said __ and

live; __ wast-in' our time __ on cheap talk and wine

The Best of My Love - 5 - 1

The Best of My Love - 5 - 4

The Best of My Love - 5 - 5

CELEBRATE ME HOME

Words by
KENNY LOGGINS

Music by
KENNY LOGGINS and
BOB JAMES

Celebrate Me Home - 5 - 1

Celebrate Me Home - 5 - 3

194

DANNY'S SONG

Words and Music by
KENNY LOGGINS

Danny's Song - 5 - 1

Danny's Song - 5 - 2

Danny's Song - 5 - 3

Danny's Song - 5 - 4

A HORSE WITH NO NAME

Words and Music by
DEWEY BUNNELL

A Horse with No Name - 5 - 3

204

A Horse with No Name - 5 - 5

AGAINST ALL ODDS
(Take a Look at Me Now)

Words and Music by
PHIL COLLINS

Against All Odds - 3 - 1

Against All Odds - 3 - 2

I _ I've got_ to face._Take a good look at me now._

I've got to take.__

Take a look at me now.__

Verse 2:
How can you just walk away from me,
When all I can do is watch you leave?
'Cause we shared the laughter and the pain,
We even shared the tears.
You're the only one who really knew me at all.
(To Chorus:)

Verse 3:
I wish I could just make you turn around,
Turn around and see me cryin',
There's so much I need to say to you,
So many reasons why.
You're the only one who really knew me at all.
(To Chorus:)

HOW SWEET IT IS
(TO BE LOVED BY YOU)

Words and Music by
EDDIE HOLLAND, LAMONT DOZIER
and BRIAN HOLLAND

211

How Sweet It Is (To Be Loved by You) - 3 - 3

HOTEL CALIFORNIA

Words and Music by
DON HENLEY, GLENN FREY
and DON FELDER

On a dark des-ert high-way,   cool wind in my
Her mind is Tif-fa-ny twist-ed.   She got the Mer-ce-des

Hotel California - 7 - 1

Hotel California - 7 - 2

I NEED YOU

Words and Music by
GERRY BECKLEY

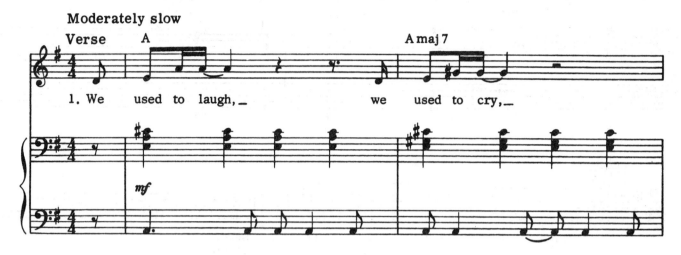

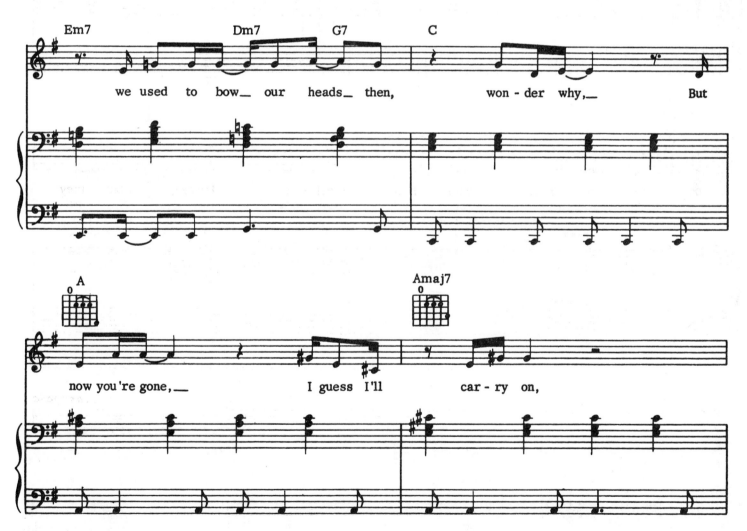

I Need You - 5 - 1

LIGHT MY FIRE

Words and Music by
THE DOORS

1. You know that it would be un - true;
2. (The) time to hes - i - tate is through,

You know that I would be a liar;
No time to wal - low in the mire,

If I was to say___ to you;___
Try now we can on - ly lose,___

And our

Light My Fire - 3 - 1

Light My Fire - 3 - 2

BOTH SIDES OF THE STORY

By PHIL COLLINS

See Block Lyrics for Verses 2,3&4

Both Sides of the Story - 7 - 1

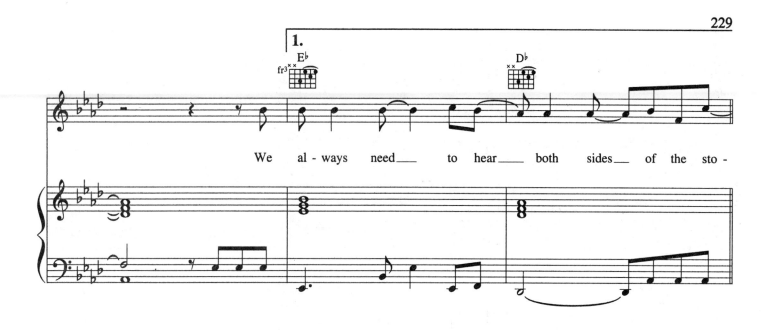

We al-ways need___ to hear___ both sides___ of the sto-

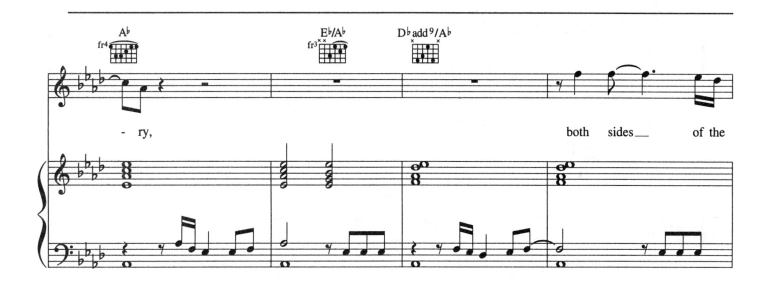

- ry, both sides___ of the

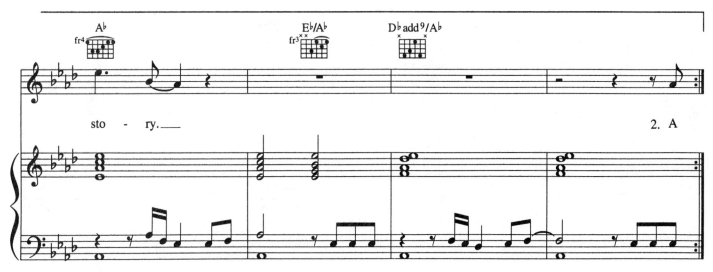

sto - ry.___

2. A

fail them now,___ be sure,___ be - fore___ we close___ our eyes,___

don't walk a - way from___ here_____ 'til you

hear___ both sides,___ no, no, no, no._____
see___ both sides,___

Both Sides of the Story - 7 - 5

Verse 2:

A neighbourhood peace is shattered, it's the middle of the night
Young faces hide in the shadows, while they watch their mother and father fight
He says she's been unfaithful, she says her love for him has gone
And the brother shrugs to his sister, and says "Looks like it's just us from now on".

Verse 3:

Here we are all gathered in what seems to be the centre of the storm
Neighbours once friendly now stand each side of the line that has been drawn
They've been fighting here for years, but now there's killing on the streets
While small coffins are lined up sadly, now united in defeat.

Verse 4:

White man turns the corner, finds himself within a different world
Ghetto kid grabs his shoulder, throws him up against the wall
He says "Would you respect me if I didn't have this gun
'Cos without it, I don't get it, and that's why I carry one".

LONESOME LOSER

Words and Music by
DAVID BRIGGS

Have you heard____ a - bout the lone - some los ____ - er, beat - en by____

____ the Queen of Hearts ev - 'ry time?____ Have you heard____ a - bout the lone - some los -

- er? He's a los - er, but he still keeps on try ___ ing.

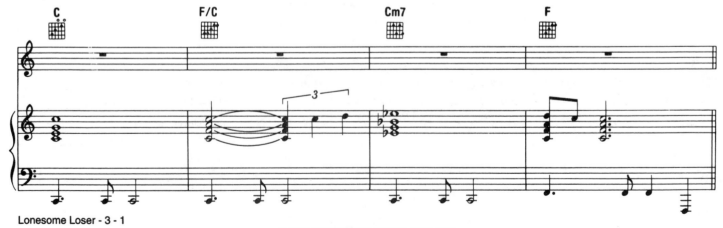

Lonesome Loser - 3 - 1

236

Lonesome Loser - 3 - 3

LIFE IN THE FAST LANE

Words and Music by
DON HENLEY, GLENN FREY & JOE WALSH

Moderate Rock beat
Tacet

He was a

hard-head-ed man.___ He was bru-tal-ly hand-some,
Ea-ger for ac-tion and hot for the game,___ the

and she was ter-mi-nal-ly pret-ty.
com-ing at-trac-tion, the drop of a name.___ They knew

Life in the Fast Lane - 7 - 1

said he was ruth-less;   they   said he was   crude.___   They had
tend-ed not to no-tice;   she was   caught up in   the___ race.

one thing in com-mon: they were good in   bed.___ She'd say,
Out ev-'ry eve-ning   un-til it   was light, he was

"Fast - er, fast - er.   The   lights are turn-in' red."___
too tired to make__ it; she was   too tired to fight a-bout it.

Life in the fast_ lane surely make_ you lose_ your mind.__

Life in the fast_ lane, mm.__

Are you with-me so far?

Life in the fast_ lane; ev-'ry-thing_ all the time.___

NEW YORK MINUTE

Words and Music by
DON HENLEY, DANNY KORTCHMAR
and JAI WINDING

Slowly, with a heavy beat

1. Har - ry got up dressed all in black,
4. I pulled my coat a - round my shoul - ders and took a walk down through the park.

New York Minute - 7 - 1

New York min- ute.

And in these days

when dark- ness falls_ ear - ly, and peo - ple rush home

to the ones they love_ you bet - ter take a fools_ ad - vice

and take care of your ___ own.

'Cause one day they're here, ___ next day they're

gone. *(Muted trumpet solo - ad lib.)*

D.S. 𝄋 *al Coda* ⊕

99

Words and Music by
DAVID PAICH

Nine - ty - nine,   I've been wait - ing __ so   long. __
Nine - ty - nine,   I keep break - ing __ your   heart. __

99 - 5 - 1

I WISH IT WOULD RAIN DOWN

Words and Music by
PHIL COLLINS

I Wish It Would Rain - 5 - 1

258

I Wish It Would Rain - 5 - 5

VERSE 2:
You said you didn't need me in your life,
Oh I guess you were right,
Ooh I never meant to cause you no pain,
But it looks like I did it again.

VERSE 3:
'Cos I know, I know I never meant to cause you no pain,
And I realise I let you down,
But I know in my heart of hearts,
I know I'm never gonna hold you again.

OPEN ARMS

Words and Music by
STEVE PERRY and JONATHAN CAIN

Open Arms - 3 - 1

Verse 3:
Living without you; living alone,
This empty house seems so cold.

Verse 4:
Wanting to hold you, wanting you near;
How much I wanted you home.

Bridge:
But now that you've come back;
Turned night into day;
I need you to stay.
(Chorus)

Open Arms - 3 - 3

PEACEFUL EASY FEELING

Words and Music by
JACK TEMPCHIN

Peaceful Easy Feeling - 6 - 1

Peaceful Easy Feeling - 6 - 2

Peaceful Easy Feeling - 6 - 4

Peaceful Easy Feeling - 6 - 6

REMINISCING

Words and Music by
GRAHAM GOBLE

Reminiscing - 5 - 1

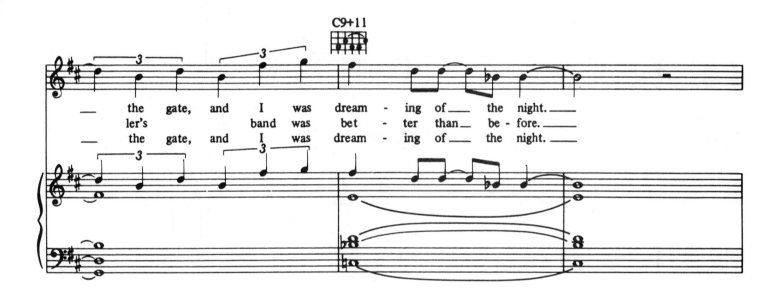

272

Reminiscing - 5 - 3

274

Reminiscing - 5 - 5

ROCK ME ON THE WATER

Words and Music by
JACKSON BROWNE

Rock Me on the Water - 5 - 3

ROSANNA

Words and Music by
DAVID PAICH

Rosanna - 5 - 1

I did-n't know you were look-in' for more_ than I could ev-er be.
I nev-er thought that __ los-in'__ you__ could ev-er hurt so bad.

Not quite a year ____ since you

went a-way,_ Ro-san - na,_____ yeah._

Now she's gone, and I

Rosanna - 5 - 4

SANDMAN

Words and Music by
DEWEY BUNNELL

SEPARATE LIVES
(Love Theme from "WHITE NIGHTS")

Words and Music by
STEPHEN BISHOP

Separate Lives - 7 - 1

Separate Lives - 7 - 2

Separate Lives - 7 - 6

SUGAR MAGNOLIA

Music by
BOB WEIR

Words by
ROBERT HUNTER and BOB WEIR

Sugar Magnolia - 9 - 1

Sugar Magnolia - 9 - 3

Su - gar Mag - no - lia, ring - ing that blue - bell,

caught up in sun - light.

Come on out sing - ing, I'll walk __ you in the sun - shine.

D. S. ℅ *al Coda* ⊕

Come on, hon - ey, come a - long with me.

Sugar Magnolia - 9 - 8

TAKE IT TO THE LIMIT

Words and Music by
RANDY MEISNER, DON HENLEY &
GLENN FREY

Take It to the Limit - 3 - 1

306

THE END OF THE INNOCENCE

Words and Music by
DON HENLEY and B.R. HORNSBY

Re- mem- ber when_ the days_
beau- ti- ful,_ for spac-
Who knows how_ long this_

The End of the Innocence - 7 - 1

The End of the Innocence - 7 - 7

THE PRETENDER

Words and Music by
JACKSON BROWNE

The Pretender - 9 - 1

The Pretender - 9 - 2

morn - ing light   comes stream - ing   in,   I'll get up and do it a -
morn - ing light   comes stream - ing   in,   you'll get up and do it a -
morn - ing light   comes stream - ing   in,   we'll get up and do it a -

To Coda ⊕   **1.**

gain.   A - men.   Say it a - gain.__   A - men.   I want to
gain.   A -
gain.

2.

men.   Caught __ be - tween the

long - ing___   for love and the   strug - gle for the   le - gal ten - der,___

The Pretender - 9 - 6

SOMETHING HAPPENED
ON THE WAY TO HEAVEN

Words and Music by
PHIL COLLINS and
DARYL STEURMER

1. & 4. We had a life,   we   had a love,
See lyrics for verses 2 & 3

Something Happened on the Way to Heaven - 7 - 1

Something Happened on the Way to Heaven - 7 - 3

Something Happened on the Way to Heaven - 7 - 5

VERSE 2:
How can something so good, go so bad,
How can something so right, go so wrong,
I don't know, I don't have all the answers,
But I want you back,
How many times can I say I'm sorry.
(How many times.)

VERSE 3:
I only wanted you as someone to love,
But something happened on the way to heaven,
It got a hold of me, and wouldn't let go,
And I want you back,
How many times can I say I'm sorry.
(How many times) yes I'm sorry (sorry.)

WHO'S CRYING NOW

Words and Music by
STEVE PERRY and JONATHAN CAIN

1. It's been a mys-ter-y,_____ and still they
2. Caught on a one-way street,_ the taste of
3. 4. *(see additional lyrics)*

try to see____ why some-thing good can hurt____ so____ bad.___
bit-ter-sweet;____ love will sur-vive some-how,____ some -

Who's Crying Now - 3 - 1

Who's Crying Now - 3 - 3

Verse 3:
So many stormy nights,
So many wrongs or rights;
Neither could change their headstrong ways.

Verse 4:
And in a lover's rage,
They tore another page.
The fighting is worth the love they save.

THIS IS IT

Words and Music by
KENNY LOGGINS and
MICHAEL McDONALD

There been times in my life ___

I've spent won-der-ing why.

Still ___ some-how I be-lieved ___

This Is It - 9 - 1

338

This Is It - 9 - 6

Repeat and fade

TEQUILA SUNRISE

Words and Music by
DON HENLEY & GLENN FREY

Tequila Sunrise - 5 - 1

She was-n't just an-oth-er wom-an and I could-n't

keep from com-in' on,___ it's been so long.___

Oh,___ and it's a hol-low feel-in', when it comes

down to deal-in'___ friends, it nev-er ends.___

TIN MAN

Words and Music by
DEWEY BUNNELL

Tin Man - 5 - 1

Tin Man - 5 - 5

TIME IN A BOTTLE

Words and Music by
JIM CROCE

Time in a Bottle - 3 - 1

Time in a Bottle - 3 - 2

WATCHING THE RIVER RUN

Words and Music by
JIM MESSINA and KENNY LOGGINS

Watching the River Run - 5 - 1

356

Watching the River Run - 5 - 5

WHILE YOU SEE A CHANCE

Lyrics by
WILL JENNINGS

Music by
STEVE WINWOOD

Very Slowly, Freely

While You See A Chance - 5 - 1

Stand up___ in **a** clear___ blue morn – ing, un – til___ you see___

___ what can be;___ **a** - lone___ in **a** cold___ day dawn – ing,

are you___ still free;___ can___ you be?___

When some cold to-mor-row finds__ you; when some sad old dream re-minds__
When there's no one left__ to leave__ you; e - ven you don't quite be-lieve__
And that old, grey wind__ is blow- ing; and there's noth-ing left worth know-

__ you how the end - less road__ un-winds__ you;
__ you; that's when noth - ing can__ de - ceive__ you; } while you see__
ing; and it's time_____ you should__ be go - ing;

mp

cresc.

While You See A Chance - 5 - 5

WHENEVER I CALL YOU "FRIEND"

Words by
KENNY LOGGINS
and MELISSA MANCHESTER

Music by
KENNY LOGGINS

Moderately, with feeling

When-ev - er I call you "friend," _ I be-gin _ to think I un - der-stand _ an - y -thing we are. You _ and I have al - ways been _ ev - er and ev - er. I see my-self with-

Whenever I Call You "Friend" - 5 - 1

Whenever I Call You "Friend" - 5 - 3

Whenever I Call You "Friend" - 5 - 4

Whenever I Call You "Friend" - 5 - 5

VENTURA HIGHWAY

Words and Music by
DEWEY BUNNELL

Chew-ing on a piece of grass, walk-ing down the _____

Ventura Highway - 7 - 1

Ventura Highway - 7 - 2

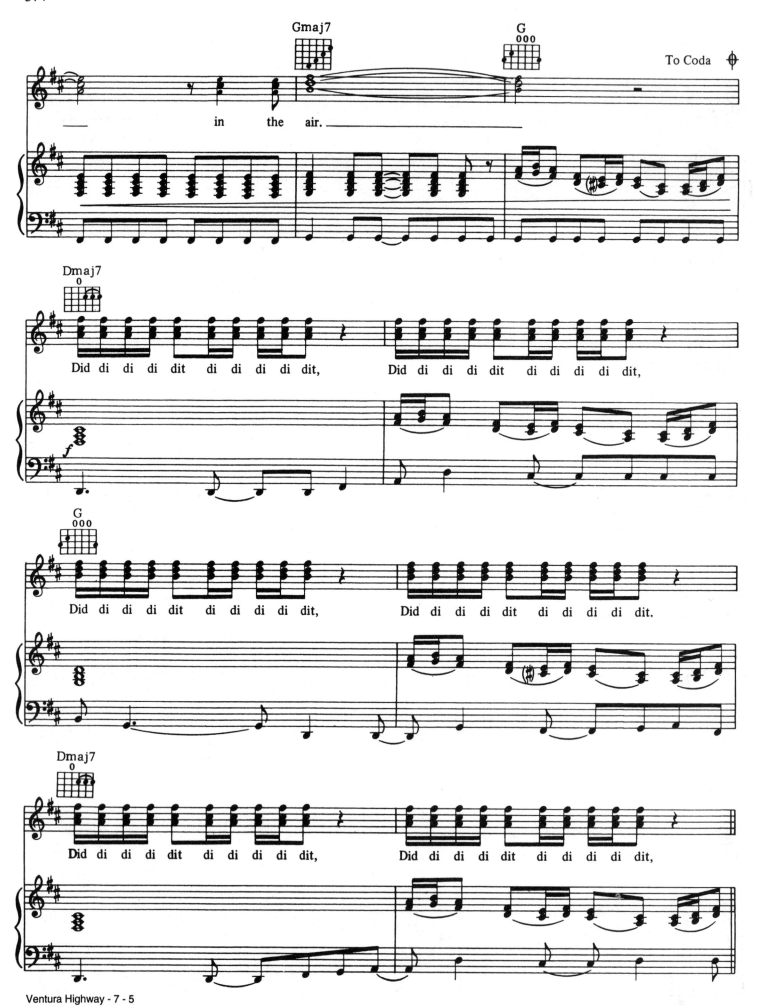

Ventura Highway - 7 - 6

change_____ your name.___

Thanks__ a lot,__

son, just the same.

D. S. al Coda

Coda

Repeat and fade

Did di di di dit di di di di dit,

Did di di di dit di di di di dit,

Did di di di dit di di di di dit,

Did di di di dit di di di di dit.

THESE DAYS

Words and Music by
JACKSON BROWNE

These Days - 3 - 1

These Days - 3 - 3

SEND HER MY LOVE

Words and Music by
STEVE PERRY and JONATHAN CAIN

Send Her My Love - 5 - 1

Instrumental Solo ad lib.

Send her, send — her my — love; —

ros - es nev - er fade. —

384

Mem - o - ries ___ re - main; ___

___ ___ send ___

___ her, send ___ her my ___ love. ___

Send Her My Love - 5 - 5

Verse 2:
The same hotel, the same old room;
I'm on the road again.
She needed so much more
Than I could give.
We knew our love could not pretend.
Broken hearts can always mend.

(To chorus:)

SUSSUDIO

Words and Music by
PHIL COLLINS

Sussudio - 5 - 1

- i -o.
- i -o.

Oh   oh.
Oh   oh.

Now she don't ev - en know my   name _____   but I
Ooh give me a chance, give me a   sign _____

think she likes me just   the   same _____   sus - sus - sud - i - o _____
I'll show her an - y time _____   sus - sus - sud - i - o _____

oh   oh.
oh   oh.

Sussudio - 5 - 3

word oh _____ sus - sus - sud - i - o _____

Showstoppers

100 or more titles in each volume of this Best-Selling Series!

Piano/Vocal/Chords:
20's, 30's, & 40's SHOWSTOPPERS
(F2865SMX)

100 nostalgic favorites include: Chattanooga Choo Choo ● Pennsylvania 6-5000 ● Blue Moon ● Moonglow ● My Blue Heaven ● Ain't Misbehavin' ● That Old Black Magic and more.

50's & 60's SHOWSTOPPERS
(F2864SMB)

Bop back to a simpler time and enjoy: Aquarius/Let the Sunshine In ● (Sittin' On) The Dock of the Bay ● Hey, Good Lookin' ● Sunny ● Johnny Angel and more.

70's & 80's SHOWSTOPPERS
P/V/C (F2863SME)
Easy Piano (F2863P2X)

100 pop songs from two decades. Titles include: Anything for You ● Blue Bayou ● Hungry Eyes ● I Wanna Dance with Somebody (Who Loves Me) ● If You Say My Eyes Are Beautiful ● I'll Never Love This Way Again ● Isn't She Lovely ● Old Time Rock & Roll ● When the Night Comes.

BIG NOTE PIANO SHOWSTOPPERS
Vol. 1 (F2871P3C)   Vol. 2 (F2918P3A)

Easy-to-read big note arrangements of 100 popular tunes include: Do You Want to Know a Secret? ● If Ever You're in My Arms Again ● Moon River ● Over the Rainbow ● Singin' in the Rain ● You Light Up My Life ● Theme from *Love Story*.

BROADWAY SHOWSTOPPERS
(F2878SMB)

100 great show tunes include: Ain't Misbehavin' ● Almost Like Being in Love ● Consider Yourself ● Give My Regards to Broadway ● Good Morning Starshine ● Mood Indigo ● Send in the Clowns ● Tomorrow.

CHRISTMAS SHOWSTOPPERS
P/V/C (F2868SMA)
Easy Piano (F2924P2X)
Big Note (F2925P3X)

100 favorite holiday songs including: Sleigh Ride ● Silver Bells ● Deck the Halls ● Have Yourself a Merry Little Christmas ● Here Comes Santa Claus ● Little Drummer Boy ● Let It Snow! Let It Snow! Let It Snow!

CLASSICAL PIANO SHOWSTOPPERS
(F2872P9X)

100 classical intermediate piano solos include: Arioso ● Bridal Chorus (from *Lohengrin*) ● Clair de Lune ● Fifth Symphony (Theme) ● Minuet in G ● Moonlight Sonata (1st Movement) ● Polovetsian Dance (from *Prince Igor*) ● The Swan ● Wedding March (from *A Midsummer Night's Dream*).

COUNTRY SHOWSTOPPERS
(F2902SMC)

A fine collection of 101 favorite country classics and standards including: Cold, Cold Heart ● For the Good Times ● I'm So Lonesome I Could Cry ● There's a Tear in My Beer ● Young Country and more.

EASY GUITAR SHOWSTOPPERS
(F2934EGA)

100 guitar arrangements of new chart hits, old favorites, classics and solid gold songs. Includes melody, chords and lyrics for songs like: Didn't We ● Love Theme from *St. Elmo's Fire* (For Just a Moment) ● Out Here on My Own ● Please Mr. Postman ● Proud Mary ● The Way He Makes Me Feel ● With You I'm Born Again ● You're the Inspiration.

EASY LISTENING SHOWSTOPPERS
(F3069SMX)

85 easy listening songs including popular favorites, standards, TV and movie selections like: After All (Love Theme from *Chances Are)* ● From a Distance ● The Greatest Love of All ● Here We Are ● Theme from *Ice Castles* (Through the Eyes of Love) ● The Vows Go Unbroken (Always True to You) ● You Are So Beautiful.

EASY ORGAN SHOWSTOPPERS
(F2873EOB)

100 great current hits and timeless standards in easy arrangements for organ include: After the Lovin' ● Always and Forever ● Come Saturday Morning ● I Just Called to Say I Love You ● Isn't She Lovely ● On the Wings of Love ● Up Where We Belong ● You Light Up My Life.

EASY PIANO SHOWSTOPPERS
Vol. 1 (F2875P2D)   Vol. 2 (F2912P2C)

100 easy piano arrangements of familiar songs include: Alfie ● Baby Elephant Walk ● Classical Gas ● Don't Cry Out Loud ● Colour My World ● The Pink Panther ● I Honestly Love You.

JAZZ SHOWSTOPPERS
(F2953SMX)

101 standard jazz tunes including: Misty ● Elmer's Tune ● Birth of the Blues ● It Don't Mean a Thing (If It Ain't Got That Swing).

MOVIE SHOWSTOPPERS
(F2866SMC)

100 songs from memorable motion pictures include: Axel F ● Up Where We Belong ● Speak Softly Love (from *The Godfather)* ● The Entertainer ● Fame ● Nine to Five ● Nobody Does It Better.

POPULAR PIANO SHOWSTOPPERS
(F2876P9B)

100 popular intermediate piano solos include: Baby Elephant Walk ● Gonna Fly Now (Theme from *Rocky)* ● The Hill Street Blues Theme ● Love Is a Many-Splendored Thing ● (Love Theme from) *Romeo and Juliet* ● Separate Lives (Love Theme from *White Nights)* ● The Shadow of Your Smile ● Theme from *The Apartment* ● Theme from *New York, New York*.

RAGTIME SHOWSTOPPERS
(F2867SMX)

These 100 original classic rags by Scott Joplin, James Scott, Joseph Lamb and other ragtime composers include: Maple Leaf Rag ● The Entertainer ● Kansas City Rag ● Ma Rag Time Baby ● The St. Louis Rag ● World's Fair Rag and many others.

ROMANTIC SHOWSTOPPERS
(F2870SMC)

101 beautiful songs including: After All (Love Theme from *Chances Are)* ● Here and Now ● I Can't Stop Loving You ● If You Say My Eyes Are Beautiful ● The Vows Go Unbroken (Always True to You) ● You Got It.

TELEVISION SHOWSTOPPERS
(F2874SMC)

103 TV themes including: Another World ● Dear John ● Hall or Nothing (The Arsenio Hall Show) ● Star Trek -The Next Generation (Main Title) ● Theme from "Cheers" (Where Everybody Knows Your Name).

The Book of *Golden* Series

**THE BOOK OF GOLDEN
ALL-TIME FAVORITES**
(F2939SMX) Piano/Vocal/Chords

**THE BOOK OF GOLDEN
BIG BAND FAVORITES**
(F3172SMX) Piano/Vocal/Chords

**THE BOOK OF GOLDEN
BROADWAY**
(F2986SMX) Piano/Vocal/Chords

**THE NEW BOOK OF GOLDEN
CHRISTMAS**
(F2478SMB) Piano/Vocal/Chords
(F2478EOX) Easy Organ
(F2478COX) Chord Organ

**THE BOOK OF GOLDEN
COUNTRY MUSIC**
(F2926SMA) Piano/Vocal/Chords

**THE BOOK OF GOLDEN
HAWAIIAN SONGS**
(F3113SMX) Piano/Vocal/Chords

**THE BOOK OF GOLDEN
IRISH SONGS**
(F3212SMX) Piano/Vocal/Chords

**THE BOOK OF GOLDEN
ITALIAN SONGS**
(F2907SMX) Piano/Vocal/Chords

THE BOOK OF GOLDEN JAZZ
(F3012SMX) Piano/Vocal/Chords

**THE NEW BOOK OF GOLDEN
LATIN SONGS**
(F3049SMX) Piano/Vocal/Chords

**THE NEW BOOK OF GOLDEN
LOVE SONGS**
(F2415SOX) Organ

**THE BOOK OF GOLDEN
MOTOWN SONGS**
(F3144SMX) Piano/Vocal/Chords

**THE NEW BOOK OF GOLDEN
MOVIE THEMES, Volume 1**
(F2810SMX) Piano/Vocal/Chords

**THE NEW BOOK OF GOLDEN
MOVIE THEMES, Volume 2**
(F2811SMX) Piano/Vocal/Chords

**THE BOOK OF GOLDEN
POPULAR FAVORITES**
(F2233SMX) Piano/Vocal/Chords

**THE BOOK OF GOLDEN
POPULAR PIANO SOLOS**
(F3193P9X) Intermediate/
Advanced Piano

**THE BOOK OF GOLDEN
ROCK 'N' ROLL**
(F2830SMB) Piano/Vocal/Chords

**THE NEW BOOK OF GOLDEN
WEDDING SONGS**
(F2265SMA) Piano/Vocal/Chords

The Legendary Performer Series
The Music of America

Piano/Vocal/Chords collections

SUSSUDIO

Words and Music by
PHIL COLLINS

Sussudio - 5 - 1

Showstoppers

100 or more titles in each volume of this Best-Selling Series!

Piano/Vocal/Chords:
20's, 30's, & 40's SHOWSTOPPERS
(F2865SMX)

100 nostalgic favorites include: Chattanooga Choo Choo • Pennsylvania 6-5000 • Blue Moon • Moonglow • My Blue Heaven • Ain't Misbehavin' • That Old Black Magic and more.

50's & 60's SHOWSTOPPERS
(F2864SMB)

Bop back to a simpler time and enjoy: Aquarius/Let the Sunshine In • (Sittin' On) The Dock of the Bay • Hey, Good Lookin' • Sunny • Johnny Angel and more.

70's & 80's SHOWSTOPPERS
P/V/C (F2863SME)
Easy Piano (F2863P2X)

100 pop songs from two decades. Titles include: Anything for You • Blue Bayou • Hungry Eyes • I Wanna Dance with Somebody (Who Loves Me) • If You Say My Eyes Are Beautiful • I'll Never Love This Way Again • Isn't She Lovely • Old Time Rock & Roll • When the Night Comes.

BIG NOTE PIANO SHOWSTOPPERS
Vol. 1 (F2871P3C)   Vol. 2 (F2918P3A)

Easy-to-read big note arrangements of 100 popular tunes include: Do You Want to Know a Secret? • If Ever You're in My Arms Again • Moon River • Over the Rainbow • Singin' in the Rain • You Light Up My Life • Theme from *Love Story*.

BROADWAY SHOWSTOPPERS
(F2878SMB)

100 great show tunes include: Ain't Misbehavin' • Almost Like Being in Love • Consider Yourself • Give My Regards to Broadway • Good Morning Starshine • Mood Indigo • Send in the Clowns • Tomorrow.

CHRISTMAS SHOWSTOPPERS
P/V/C (F2868SMA)
Easy Piano (F2924P2X)
Big Note (F2925P3X)

100 favorite holiday songs including: Sleigh Ride • Silver Bells • Deck the Halls • Have Yourself a Merry Little Christmas • Here Comes Santa Claus • Little Drummer Boy • Let It Snow! Let It Snow! Let It Snow!

CLASSICAL PIANO SHOWSTOPPERS
(F2872P9X)

100 classical intermediate piano solos include: Arioso • Bridal Chorus (from *Lohengrin*) • Clair de Lune • Fifth Symphony (Theme) • Minuet in G • Moonlight Sonata (1st Movement) • Polovetsian Dance (from *Prince Igor*) • The Swan • Wedding March (from *A Midsummer Night's Dream*).

COUNTRY SHOWSTOPPERS
(F2902SMC)

A fine collection of 101 favorite country classics and standards including: Cold, Cold Heart • For the Good Times • I'm So Lonesome I Could Cry • There's a Tear in My Beer • Young Country and more.

EASY GUITAR SHOWSTOPPERS
(F2934EGA)

100 guitar arrangements of new chart hits, old favorites, classics and solid gold songs. Includes melody, chords and lyrics for songs like: Didn't We • Love Theme from *St. Elmo's Fire* (For Just a Moment) • Out Here on My Own • Please Mr. Postman • Proud Mary • The Way He Makes Me Feel • With You I'm Born Again • You're the Inspiration.

EASY LISTENING SHOWSTOPPERS
(F3069SMX)

85 easy listening songs including popular favorites, standards, TV and movie selections like: After All (Love Theme from *Chances Are*) • From a Distance • The Greatest Love of All • Here We Are • Theme from *Ice Castles* (Through the Eyes of Love) • The Vows Go Unbroken (Always True to You) • You Are So Beautiful.

EASY ORGAN SHOWSTOPPERS
(F2873EOB)

100 great current hits and timeless standards in easy arrangements for organ include: After the Lovin' • Always and Forever • Come Saturday Morning • I Just Called to Say I Love You • Isn't She Lovely • On the Wings of Love • Up Where We Belong • You Light Up My Life.

EASY PIANO SHOWSTOPPERS
Vol. 1 (F2875P2D)   Vol. 2 (F2912P2C)

100 easy piano arrangements of familiar songs include: Alfie • Baby Elephant Walk • Classical Gas • Don't Cry Out Loud • Colour My World • The Pink Panther • I Honestly Love You.

JAZZ SHOWSTOPPERS
(F2953SMX)

101 standard jazz tunes including: Misty • Elmer's Tune • Birth of the Blues • It Don't Mean a Thing (If It Ain't Got That Swing).

MOVIE SHOWSTOPPERS
(F2866SMC)

100 songs from memorable motion pictures include: Axel F • Up Where We Belong • Speak Softly Love (from *The Godfather)* • The Entertainer • Fame • Nine to Five • Nobody Does It Better.

POPULAR PIANO SHOWSTOPPERS
(F2876P9B)

100 popular intermediate piano solos include: Baby Elephant Walk • Gonna Fly Now (Theme from *Rocky*) • The Hill Street Blues Theme • Love Is a Many-Splendored Thing • (Love Theme from) *Romeo and Juliet* • Separate Lives (Love Theme from *White Nights*) • The Shadow of Your Smile • Theme from *The Apartment* • Theme from *New York, New York*.

RAGTIME SHOWSTOPPERS
(F2867SMX)

These 100 original classic rags by Scott Joplin, James Scott, Joseph Lamb and other ragtime composers include: Maple Leaf Rag • The Entertainer • Kansas City Rag • Ma Rag Time Baby • The St. Louis Rag • World's Fair Rag and many others.

ROMANTIC SHOWSTOPPERS
(F2870SMC)

101 beautiful songs including: After All (Love Theme from *Chances Are*) • Here and Now • I Can't Stop Loving You • If You Say My Eyes Are Beautiful • The Vows Go Unbroken (Always True to You) • You Got It.

TELEVISION SHOWSTOPPERS
(F2874SMC)

103 TV themes including: Another World • Dear John • Hall or Nothing (The Arsenio Hall Show) • Star Trek -The Next Generation (Main Title) • Theme from "Cheers" (Where Everybody Knows Your Name).

The Book of *Golden* Series

THE BOOK OF GOLDEN ALL-TIME FAVORITES
(F2939SMX) Piano/Vocal/Chords

THE BOOK OF GOLDEN BIG BAND FAVORITES
(F3172SMX) Piano/Vocal/Chords

THE BOOK OF GOLDEN BROADWAY
(F2986SMX) Piano/Vocal/Chords

THE NEW BOOK OF GOLDEN CHRISTMAS
(F2478SMB) Piano/Vocal/Chords
(F2478EOX) Easy Organ
(F2478COX) Chord Organ

THE BOOK OF GOLDEN COUNTRY MUSIC
(F2926SMA) Piano/Vocal/Chords

THE BOOK OF GOLDEN HAWAIIAN SONGS
(F3113SMX) Piano/Vocal/Chords

THE BOOK OF GOLDEN IRISH SONGS
(F3212SMX) Piano/Vocal/Chords

THE BOOK OF GOLDEN ITALIAN SONGS
(F2907SMX) Piano/Vocal/Chords

THE BOOK OF GOLDEN JAZZ
(F3012SMX) Piano/Vocal/Chords

THE NEW BOOK OF GOLDEN LATIN SONGS
(F3049SMX) Piano/Vocal/Chords

THE NEW BOOK OF GOLDEN LOVE SONGS
(F2415SOX) Organ

THE BOOK OF GOLDEN MOTOWN SONGS
(F3144SMX) Piano/Vocal/Chords

THE NEW BOOK OF GOLDEN MOVIE THEMES, Volume 1
(F2810SMX) Piano/Vocal/Chords

THE NEW BOOK OF GOLDEN MOVIE THEMES, Volume 2
(F2811SMX) Piano/Vocal/Chords

THE BOOK OF GOLDEN POPULAR FAVORITES
(F2233SMX) Piano/Vocal/Chords

THE BOOK OF GOLDEN POPULAR PIANO SOLOS
(F3193P9X) Intermediate/
Advanced Piano

THE BOOK OF GOLDEN ROCK 'N' ROLL
(F2830SMB) Piano/Vocal/Chords

THE NEW BOOK OF GOLDEN WEDDING SONGS
(F2265SMA) Piano/Vocal/Chords

The Legendary Performer Series
The Music of America

Piano/Vocal/Chords collections